For Rob and all the amazing dads out there.

-C.M.

To Lani and Jack, who brighten the colors of my world every day.

-E.M.

94-411 Kōʻaki Street
Waipahu, Hawaiʻi 96797-2806
Orders: (800) 468-2800
Information: (808) 564-8800
Fax: (808) 564-8877
welcometotheislands.com
COP: 191103

ISBN: 1-61710-407-8
First Edition, First Printing–2019

Pu'ulei and the Everyday Rainbow

Written by Crissy Miyake
Illustrated by Erin Makai

ISLAND HERITAGE™

On the island of O'ahu, in a grassy field near the world-renowned Diamond Head crater, lived a Daddy pueo and his daughter, Pu'ulei.

Pu'ulei was special. She had unique feathers around her neck that made it look like she was wearing a beautiful lei. In fact, she was given the name Pu'ulei because of these unusual markings.

As Hawaiian pueo, Pu'ulei and her Daddy were not nocturnal like other owls. They were diurnal, most active during the daytime. Every morning Daddy would wake Pu'ulei up and every morning, Pu'ulei watched Daddy rush around.

One particularly hurried morning she asked, "Daddy, why are you always so busy?"

He hastily replied, "Oh, Pu'ulei, I have so many things to do. I need to get you to school. Then I need to find leaves and twigs to fix the nest, and find us food. After I pick you up from school I need to take you to flying lessons. Whoo-whoo! Every day there is so much to do and I have to hurry to get it all done."

HELLO
OWL
BUG BUTTER
OWL
MART
DAD

Puʻulei didn't like being rushed, but she immediately followed her Daddy out of the nest.

DA KINE FRUIT
EXPECT DELAYS
TAXI

While flying to school Daddy said, “Look down, Pu‘ulei. Do you see all those cars? All the people? Everyone is rushing around because they have so much to do, not just me.” Pu‘ulei saw all the cars, the traffic, and the people. She saw the same things she sees every day. However, she also saw something more.

Pu‘ulei replied “Daddy, I see how busy everyone is, but I also see a rainbow of colors around us. Do you see the Everyday Rainbow?”

Daddy looked perplexed. “No. I don’t see a rainbow.”

“No Daddy,” Pu‘ulei replied, “an EVERYDAY RAINBOW. It is made from all the beautiful things you see every day. If you look closely you can see everyday things in a new way and use their colors to make your own rainbow…every day. That’s an Everyday Rainbow!”

Daddy looked confused so Pu'ulei explained further. "Look down again. Do you see the pretty purple bougainvillea along the freeway? That purple is a part of my Everyday Rainbow for today."

When Daddy looked down, he only saw the traffic. Then he saw the patch of purple flowers and nodded.

Pu'ulei then asked Daddy to look up. "See the blue sky all around us? Today that will also be a part of my Everyday Rainbow."

As he looked up, Daddy saw that the sky was clear and a bright blue. He thought, "Whoo-whoo! Today will be a sunny day. It will make looking for leaves, twigs and food easier. I am thankful for that!"

SHAVE ICE
STOP

The little owl looked around and saw tall coconut trees in Waikīkī. She watched the leaves dance in the wind. “See those coconut trees, Daddy? That’s the green in my rainbow today.”

As he flew he saw coconut trees, the same ones he passed every day, but was usually too busy to notice.

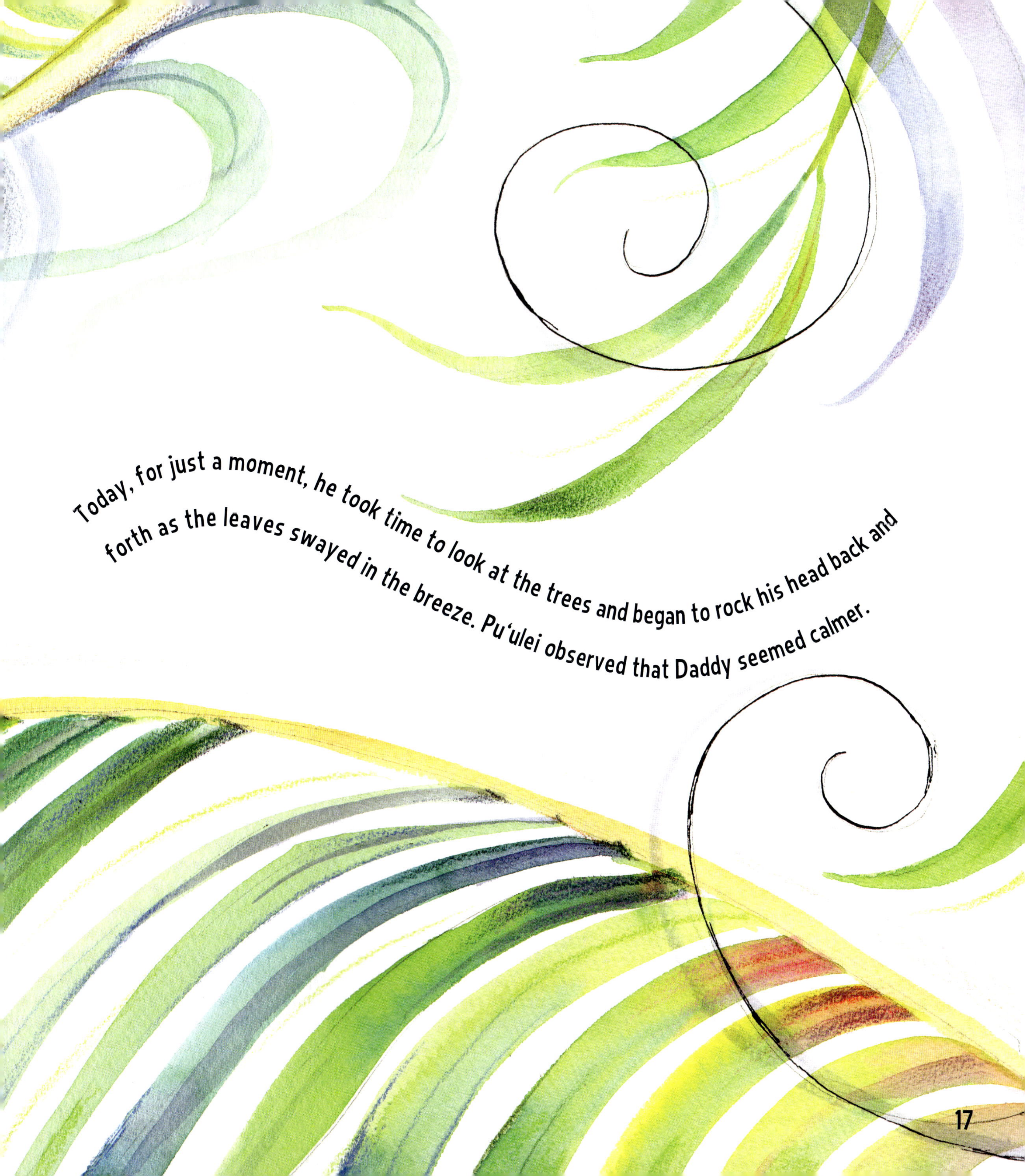

Today, for just a moment, he took time to look at the trees and began to rock his head back and forth as the leaves swayed in the breeze. Pu'ulei observed that Daddy seemed calmer.

Pu‘ulei noticed that he had stunning yellow feathers on the side of his wings. She exclaimed, “Daddy! Your beautiful golden feathers are part of my Everyday Rainbow!”

Daddy realized that Pu‘ulei was right. He did have yellow-golden feathers that were dazzling in the sunlight.

As they approached Ala Moana Beach, she asked him to look down. "Daddy, do you see the sun shining on the store windows and skyscrapers? It's such a beautiful orange glow. That's the orange in my rainbow today."

Daddy gazed at how the warm, orange color in all the windows reflected the sun and made everything look like a stunning sunrise.

As they passed Chinatown the tiny pueo said, “Look down below Daddy. Do you see the red tiles on top of the old buildings? That is the red in my rainbow today.”

This time Daddy spotted the red buildings easily, as well as other red things. Red flags flapping in the wind, red curtains covering the shop windows, and red lanterns hanging above display tables.

Daddy observed how the things he saw every day were beautiful in their own way, just as they are, even on the most hectic days. The world was a kaleidoscope of colors and he was comforted by all that surrounded him. He began to look for his Everyday Rainbow.

When they arrived at school, Pu‘ulei saw that Daddy was different. He was smiling. He looked calm and happy.

As Pu‘ulei hugged Daddy he whispered in her ear, “Mahalo Pu‘ulei for sharing your Everyday Rainbow with me. I love you.”

Daddy watched his daughter flutter into school. As he left to start running his errands he smiled because he was going to find his own Everyday Rainbow.

Glossary & Cultural Background

Pueo [pooh-eh ooh] - (singular and plural) Hawaiian owl. Pueo are believed to have arrived in the Hawaiian Islands about a thousand years ago. Pueo have a special place in traditional Hawaiian folklore and mythology as personal/familial spiritual guides or ʻaumākua. Pueo are known to be bringers of luck, protectors, and messengers. While pueo are found on each of the main Hawaiian Islands, they are considered endangered by the state of Hawaiʻi.

Inoa, or giving something a name in Hawaiian culture, has strong spiritual significance and is often connected to family history, a dream, or a vision. The Hawaiian name given often describes an individual's personality, aptitudes, skills, or physical characteristics. In the story, Puʻulei was given her name based on her traits. Puʻu [poo-ooh] - a hill, a peak, or any protrusion that sticks out (where she lives) and Lei [lay] - a necklace made of flowers, shells, seeds, nuts, leaves, feathers, bones and teeth, etc. are combined to make her name, Puʻulei.

A Note about Mindful Appreciation:

Mindful appreciation, or mindful gratitude, brings focused awareness to our immediate environment and challenges us to see every day in a new way. The goal is to see the unique beauty in our lives...just the way it is. The Everyday Rainbow teaches children to look for, and pay attention to, the positiveness that exists in their everyday lives, not the negative things.

The simple activity of seeing positivity around them can help children practice how to shift their attention/focus/energy onto what is positive and experience increased appreciation/gratitude.

There is an emerging body of research and literature that supports the therapeutic advantages of mindfulness and gratitude. Mindfully practicing gratitude increases self-esteem, resilience, improves physical health, and enhances positive emotions.